AMAZING INVENTORY OF INCREDIBLE KNOWLEDGE

PUB
TIME

TRIVIA

pil

Publications International, Ltd.

Written by **Jill Oldham**

Cover photo: **Thinkstock**

Louis Weber, CEO
Publications International, Ltd.
7373 North Cicero Avenue
Lincolnwood, Illinois 60712

ISBN-13: 978-1-4508-6025-3
ISBN-10: 1-4508-6025-7

Manufactured in China.

8 7 6 5 4 3 2 1

# CONTENTS

# TRIVIA TIME

Welcome to *Pub Time Trivia.* This is not your typical trivia book. If you're looking for dry and dusty historical trivia, you won't find it here. But if you think you know—or always wanted to know—where the world's largest ketchup bottle is located, what Homer Simpson and Elvis Presley have in common, which celebrities tweeted what, and many more fascinating facts, you've come to the right place.

*Pub Time Trivia* is organized by topic, making it easy for you to "pick your poison," so to speak. Maybe you're a sports whiz and want to kick off with Sports of All Sorts. Or perhaps you win the office Oscar pool every year and would prefer to premiere with Movie Mania. You'll find questions on the right-hand pages and answers on the back of each page, along with a few extra tidbits that may teach you a thing or two.

Are you ready? Pull up a barstool, pull out *Pub Time Trivia,* and tell your friends, "It's on."

# ANIMALS

### 1) Which of these dog breeds cannot bark?

A. Azawakh

B. Basenji

C. Catalburun

D. Mudi

### 2) Insect stings kill between 40 and 100 Americans every year. But in other parts of the world, bugs kill many times that number. Which of these critters is responsible for the most human deaths?

A. Assassin bug

B. Japanese beetle

C. Mosquito

D. Tsetse fly

B. Basenjis, a favorite dog of ancient Egyptians, are incapable of barking. Instead, you'll hear them uttering a sound called a yodel. Azawakhs (African sight hounds), catalburuns (Turkish pointers that are readily identified by their "split-nose"), and mudis (Hungarian herding dogs) all make themselves heard with traditional barks.

---

C. Believe it or not, mosquitoes are responsible for more deaths than any other creature in the world. They spread a wide variety of potentially deadly diseases, including malaria, which kills an estimated two million people a year.

## WHO KNEW?

In the Middle Ages fleas were to blame for the deaths of approximately 75 million people—nearly half the population of Europe. They transmitted the bacteria that caused the plague, or the Black Death.

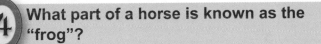

**3** **What is a capon?**

A. A castrated rooster

B. A pygmy giraffe

C. A wild dog

D. An unfertilized eagle egg

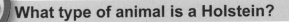

**4** **What part of a horse is known as the "frog"?**

A. Chest

B. Head

C. Hoof

D. Tail

**5** **What type of animal is a Holstein?**

A. Cow

B. Horse

C. Pig

D. Sheep

**6** **True or false: The sting from a killer bee can be fatal.**

A. Ouch. Why would a rooster be castrated? To improve the tenderness and quality of its meat. Capon is known as a luxury food.

C. The frog is the triangular mark on the bottom of a horse's hoof.

A. Got milk? Black-and-white (or sometimes red-and-white) Holsteins are the most popular dairy cows in the United States, making up 90 percent of the total herd.

True. Africanized honeybees, as killer bees are officially known, are extremely aggressive. They often attack in swarms, and their stings can kill. They are notorious for being easy to provoke and hard to escape. They will chase humans for great distances, and they've been known to stay angry for up to 24 hours.

**7** Which species contains the most poisonous animal in the world?

A. Butterfly

B. Frog

C. Snake

D. Spider

**8** Most people know that a group of lions is called a pride and a group of fish is called a school, but can you match these animals with their collective group names?

1. Apes        A. Murder

2. Crows       B. Parliament

3. Jellyfish   C. Pod

4. Owls        D. Shrewdness

5. Ravens      E. Smack

6. Whales      F. Unkindness

## WHO KNEW?

Most elephants weigh less than the tongue of a blue whale.

**7** B. Dart poison frogs are the most poisonous animals in the world. The golden poison frog is so toxic that it's dangerous to even touch it. Just one golden poison frog has enough toxin to kill ten people. So if you find yourself in Central or South America, you might want to think twice before kissing that frog.

**8** 1. D; 2. A; 3. E; 4. B; 5. F; 6. C.

## WHO KNEW?

When some types of frogs vomit, their entire stomach comes out. The frog then cleans the contents and swallows the empty stomach.

**9** Which of the following animals was never a resident of the White House?

A. Alligator

B. Bobcat

C. Ostrich

D. Pygmy hippopotamus

 **10** What is stored inside a camel's hump?

 **11** Macaroni, gentoo, chinstrap, and rockhopper are types of what?

A. Butterflies

B. Dogs

C. Penguins

D. Zebras

*"Animals are such agreeable friends—they ask no questions, they pass no criticisms."*

—George Eliot

C. The White House has been home to all sorts of animals—domesticated and otherwise. John Quincy Adams owned a gator that lived in the East Room for two months. Calvin Coolidge literally had a zoo at the White House, including a bobcat, a pygmy hippo, a bear, lion cubs, raccoons, a hyena, and more. Theodore Roosevelt had an extensive menagerie too.

Fat. If you thought the answer was water, you're not alone. (You're wrong, but you're not alone.) The fat stored in a camel's hump allows the animal to go for up to a month without food—pretty useful for those long treks across the desert.

C. There are 17 breeds of penguins in the world; these are just four of them.

**12** Which of the following is *not* a type of cat?

A. Calico

B. Rex

C. Saluki

D. Scottish Fold

 **13** Of the 12 signs of the zodiac, how many are modeled on animals?

 **14** What do snakes primarily use their tongues for?

A. Hearing

B. Seeing

C. Smelling

D. Tasting

*"You will always be lucky if you know how to make friends with strange cats."*

—American proverb

C. Salukis are dogs—in fact, theirs may be the oldest known breed of domes- ticated dog. Salukis were held in such great esteem in ancient Egypt that they were some- times mummified along with the pharaohs.

---

 Seven. Aries (ram), Taurus (bull), Cancer (crab), Leo (lion), Scorpio (scorpion), Capricorn (sea goat), and Pisces (fish) are animal signs.

---

C. Snakes can use their tongues for tast- ing and even touching, but they use them mostly for smelling.

## WHO KNEW?
Sharks have no tongues. Their taste buds are in their teeth.

# ARTS & LITERATURE

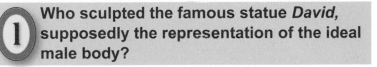

**Who sculpted the famous statue *David*, supposedly the representation of the ideal male body?**

A. Botticelli

B. Michelangelo

C. Francesco da Sangallo

D. Leonardo da Vinci

**Which author created the Land of Oz?**

A. Roald Dahl

B. J.R.R. Tolkein

C. L. Frank Baum

D. C. S. Lewis

**1** B. Take that, Mike "the Situation." You may think you have abs of steel, but David has equally well-sculpted abs of marble—and he's more than 500 years old.

**2** C. Oz stemmed from Baum's imagination, but the other writers also created some pretty fantastical worlds: Dahl came up with Willie Wonka's chocolate factory (among others), Tolkein is responsible for Middle-earth of *Lord of the Rings,* and Lewis dreamed up Narnia.

## WHO KNEW?
L. Frank Baum allegedly came up with the name Oz based on the label on a file cabinet: O–Z.

**3** **What does the "J" stand for in author J. K. Rowling's name?**

A. Jane

B. Joanne

C. Joely

D. Judy

 **4** **Oprah Winfrey famously got into a fight with which author on her talk show?**

A. Dave Eggers

B. Jonathan Franzen

C. James Frey

D. Jonathan Safran Foer

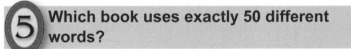 **5** **Which book uses exactly 50 different words?**

*"Books are like mirrors: If a fool looks in, you cannot expect a genius to look out."*

—J. K. Rowling

**3** B. The initials stand for Joanne Kathleen, but the *Harry Potter* author usually goes by "Jo."

**4** C. When Oprah discovered that the author of the self-purported memoir *A Million Little Pieces* had lied about parts of his life in the novel, she was outraged. She said she felt "duped" and proceeded to give him a very public verbal whoopin'.

**5** Dr. Seuss's *Green Eggs and Ham.* Seuss's editor bet him he couldn't write a book using 50 words or less. Guess what? The editor lost.

## WHO KNEW?
The first known use of the word *nerd* is in Dr. Seuss's *If I Ran the Zoo* (1956).

**6** Who designed the Guggenheim Museum in New York City?

A. Frank Gehry

B. Louis Kahn

C. Ludwig Mies van der Rohe

D. Frank Lloyd Wright

**7** On which surface would you find a traditional fresco?

A. A canvas

B. A piece of pottery

C. Skin

D. A wall

**8** Match these artists with the movement with which they are most associated:

1. Salvador Dali        A. Cubism
2. Michelangelo         B. Impressionism
3. Claude Monet         C. Pop Art
4. Pablo Picasso        D. Renaissance
5. Andy Warhol          E. Surrealism

**6** D. The renowned modern-art museum showcased both Wright's affinity for the natural world and his later take on modernist architecture. It opened in 1959, after the death of both Wright and art collector Solomon Guggenheim.

**7** D. A fresco (which means "fresh" in Italian) is a mural painted on fresh, wet plaster with natural pigments. As the plaster and paint dry, the fresco hardens and becomes permanent. Frescoes are commonly found on church walls.

 **8** 1. E; 2. D; 3. B; 4. A; 5. C.

## WHO KNEW?

*Le Bateau,* a painting by Henri Matisse, hung upside down in the Museum of Modern Art in New York for 47 days before someone realized it.

**9** Which American pop artist is known for his paintings that resemble large comic strips?

A. Keith Haring

B. David Hockney

C. Roy Lichtenstein

D. Andy Warhol

 **10** How did legendary playwright Tennessee Williams *(A Streetcar Named Desire, Cat on a Hot Tin Roof)* die?

A. He choked on a bottlecap.

B. He drowned in the Mississippi River.

C. He fell from a sixth-story window.

D. He was stabbed.

 **11** Which famous 20th-century novelist was known to many by the name "Papa"?

A. Truman Capote

B. William Faulkner

C. Ernest Hemingway

D. Kurt Vonnegut

Questions

**9** C. All four are leaders of the pop art movement, but only Lichtenstein created oversize paintings in the style of bold and bright traditional comic strips.

 **10** A. Williams, who battled alcoholism and depression for much of his life, died in 1983 at age 71 as a result of choking on the cap from a bottle of eyedrops.

**11** Ask not for whom the bell tolls; it tolls for (C), Ernest Hemingway, one of the best-known and most successful novelists of the 20th century. His works include *A Farewell to Arms, To Have and Have Not,* and, yes, *For Whom the Bell Tolls,* among others.

*"Always do sober what you said you'd do drunk. That will teach you to keep your mouth shut."*

—Ernest Hemingway

22

Which character is *not* found in *Alice in Wonderland*?

A. The Mad Hatter

B. The Mock Turtle

C. Tweedledum and Tweedledee

D. The White Witch

 According to Greek legend, what was left in Pandora's box after she opened it, releasing misery and evil into the world?

A. Faith

B. Hope

C. Innocence

D. Trust

 Who coined the phrase "15 minutes of fame"?

A. Walt Disney

B. Hugh Hefner

C. Marilyn Monroe

D. Andy Warhol

**12** D. Alice encountered the Mad Hatter, the Mock Turtle, and Tweedledum and Tweedledee on her travels through Wonderland. To bump into the White Witch, she would have needed to take a detour to the land of Narnia.

 **13** B. Tricky Zeus. The king of gods gave Pandora a box (well, technically it was a jar, but why quibble?) and warned her never, ever to open it. Of course he knew her curiosity would get the better of her, and indeed it did. Fortunately she was able to slam the lid shut while hope still remained.

 **14** D. The avant-garde pop artist said, "In the future, everybody will be world famous for 15 minutes." The phrase made its way into the popular vernacular, where it remains widely used.

**15** What color is the Arts and Literature wedge in the game Trivial Pursuit?

 **16** Who wrote *Pride and Prejudice*?

A. Jane Austen

B. Elizabeth Bennet

C. Charlotte Brontë

D. Emily Brontë

**17** Which of the following was *not* a pen name of Samuel Clemens (Mark Twain)?

A. W. Epaminondas Adrastus Blab

B. Sergeant Fathom

C. Thomas Jefferson Snodgrass

D. Milcent Mollins Stanwix

## WHO KNEW?

*Little Women* author Louisa May Alcott fought to have Mark Twain's *Huckleberry Finn* banned from public libraries, claiming it was inappropriate for "pure-minded lads and lassies."

ARTS & LITERATURE

**15** Brown. (Talk about trivial trivia!)

---

**16** A. Austen wrote the widely beloved novel. The Brontë sisters contributed *Jane Eyre* (Charlotte) and *Wuthering Heights* (Emily) to the genre. Elizabeth Bennet is a figment of Austen's imagination—the main character in *Pride and Prejudice*.

---

**17** D. The 19th-century humorist looked at life with a keen wit, and he never took himself too seriously either, as can be seen in his choice of aliases.

*"Better to keep your mouth shut and appear stupid than to open it and remove all doubt."*

—Mark Twain

# FAMOUS FIRSTS

**1** The first credit card was introduced in New York in 1950. What was it?

A. American Express

B. BankAmericard

C. Diners Club

D. MasterCard

**2** Who was the cover model of the first issue of *Playboy* magazine (1953)?

A. Brigitte Bardot

B. Sophia Loren

C. Jayne Mansfield

D. Marilyn Monroe

Questions

**1** C. Although the American Express company was established a century before Diners Club, it specialized in deliveries (as a competitor to the U.S. Postal Service), money orders, and traveler's checks. It didn't enter the credit card industry until 1958.

---

**2** D. Monroe was also the centerfold of that issue, although she did not pose nude.

## WHO KNEW?
Burt Reynolds posed for *Cosmopolitan*'s first centerfold (in 1972)—and he *was* nude.

**3** **The first moving picture copyrighted in America showed what?**

A. An automobile racing a horse

B. A lady crossing a street

C. A man sneezing

D. Two people kissing

**4** **What was the first item sold on eBay?**

A. Answering machine

B. Calculator

C. Computer keyboard

D. Laser pointer

**5** **Who was the first human in space?**

A. Yuri Gagarin

B. John Glenn

C. Alan Shepard

D. German Titov

C. The five-second movie, filmed in 1894 by the Edison Manufacturing Company (yes, *that* Edison—he did a whole lot more than just invent the lightbulb), showed Edison's assistant Fred Ott taking a pinch of snuff and sneezing. Five stars!

D. eBay was founded in 1995 by Pierre Omidyar, whose broken laser pointer was the first product to be auctioned off (reportedly for about $14). The buyer was aware it was broken— he wanted it as an addition to his collection of broken laser pointers. True story.

A. The Russian cosmonaut launched on the *Vostok 1* on April 12, 1961, and orbited the Earth once. The spacecraft was controlled from the ground for the duration of the 108-minute flight, and Gagarian was its only passenger.

**What was the first animated film to be nominated for an Oscar for Best Picture?**

A. *Aladdin*

B. *Beauty and the Beast*

C. *The Lion King*

D. *The Little Mermaid*

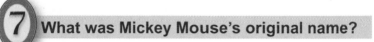 **What was Mickey Mouse's original name?**

A. Malachi Mouse

B. Marvin Mouse

C. Milton Mouse

D. Mortimer Mouse

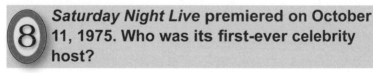 *Saturday Night Live* **premiered on October 11, 1975. Who was its first-ever celebrity host?**

A. Desi Arnaz

B. Candice Bergen

C. George Carlin

D. Bob Newhart

**6** B. *Beauty and the Beast* was nominated in 1991 but was beaten out by *The Silence of the Lambs*. However, it did win the Golden Globe for Best Picture (Musical or Comedy) that year—the first full-length animated feature to claim that prize.

**7** D. Walt Disney created Mortimer Mouse in 1928. The name was short-lived, however; supposedly Disney's wife thought it sounded too pompous and suggested "Mickey" as a replacement.

**8** C. Unlike today's guest hosts, who appear in most of the show's sketches, Carlin only appeared onstage to perform stand-up comedy and introduce the musical guests.

## 9. Can you match the celebrity with his first-ever tweet?

1. Bill Cosby
2. Danny DeVito
3. Tom Hanks
4. Neil Patrick Harris
5. Ashton Kutcher

A. dropping my first tweet

B. Have a tweet time and I will write tweet nothings in your ear.

C. I just joined Twitter! I don't really get this site or how it works. My nuts are on fire.

D. My first tweet, peeps. I apologize in advance for my slow learning curve. Nice to (sort of) meet you. It's amazing how quickly 140 charac

E. Testing... Testing... Is this thing on?

## 10. What was the first college founded in the United States?

A. College of William and Mary
B. Harvard University
C. University of Pennsylvania
D. Yale University

**9** 1. B; 2. C; 3. E; 4. D; 5. A.

**10** B. Harvard was called "New College" when it was founded in 1636. Technically, Henricus Colledge was chartered first (in Virginia in 1619), but it was a casualty of the Indian uprising of 1622.

## WHO KNEW?
Al-Azhar University in Cairo, Egypt, was founded in 988 A.D. It's generally considered to be the oldest university in the world.

**11** **What was the first selection for Oprah's Book Club?**

A. *The Deep End of the Ocean* (Jacquelyn Mitchard)

B. *Here on Earth* (Alice Hoffman)

C. *Song of Solomon* (Toni Morrison)

D. *White Oleander* (Janet Fitch)

 **12** **What was the first video ever played on MTV?**

A. "Beat It," Michael Jackson

B. "Money for Nothing," Dire Straits

C. "Paradise by the Dashboard Light," Meat Loaf

D. "Video Killed the Radio Star," The Buggles

**13** **Which First Lady was a distant cousin of her husband?**

*"The first of April is the day we remember what we are the other 364 days of the year."*

—Mark Twain

**11** A. Thanks to Oprah's influence, Mitchard's book became a national best-seller within four months of its publication.

**12** D. At midnight on August 1, 1981, MTV launched with the airing of the music video of the Buggles' 1979 debut single. Irony at its finest.

**13** Eleanor Roosevelt. She and FDR were fifth cousins once removed.

*"Great minds discuss ideas; average minds discuss events; small minds discuss people."*

—First Lady Eleanor Roosevelt

**14** Which teams played in the first Super Bowl?

A. Green Bay Packers and Oakland Raiders

B. Green Bay Packers and Kansas City Chiefs

C. Baltimore Colts and New York Jets

D. Minnesota Vikings and Kansas City Chiefs

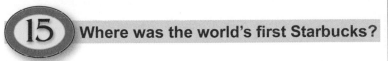 **15** Where was the world's first Starbucks?

A. Portland, Oregon

B. San Francisco, California

C. Seattle, Washington

D. Vancouver, Canada

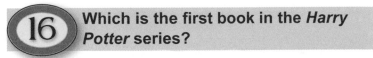 **16** Which is the first book in the *Harry Potter* series?

A. *Harry Potter and the Chamber of Secrets*

B. *Harry Potter and the Goblet of Fire*

C. *Harry Potter and the Prisoner of Azkaban*

D. *Harry Potter and the Sorcerer's Stone*

B. The first Super Bowl, called the AFL–NFL World Championship Game, was played in February 1967. The Green Bay Packers beat the Kansas City Chiefs 35–10.

---

 C. Although today it may seem like there's a Starbucks on every corner, believe it or not there was a time when you would have had to travel to Seattle to get your morning fix. When it opened in 1971, the store didn't even sell coffee by the cup; it sold small batches of fresh-roasted coffee.

---

D. If you're European, you probably know the book as *Harry Potter and the Philosopher's Stone.* Its U.S. publisher decided to rename it to emphasize the magic and wizardry—"philosopher" just didn't have the same pizzazz.

# FOOD & DRINK

**1** **What is the only food that, when sealed, doesn't spoil?**

A. Beer nuts

B. Capers

C. Fruit preserves

D. Honey

**2** **True or false: It takes seven years to digest swallowed gum.**

**3** **What does the Scoville scale measure?**

A. The fattiness of a cut of meat

B. The purity of olive oil

C. The "heat" of chilies

D. The clarity of wine

Questions

**1** D. Airtight containers will make honey last forever—literally! Several giant vats of honey, untouched for more than 3,000 years, were excavated from King Tut's tomb. Incredibly, the honey was found to still be edible.

**2** False. Even though gum is indigestible, it still passes through your digestive system at a normal rate.

**3** C. Are you feeling hot, hot, hot? The Scoville scale can either confirm or refute your hotness.

## WHO KNEW?
According to Guinness World Records, the hottest pepper in the world is called the Trinidad Scorpion Butch T and comes from Australia.

**4** The McDonald's Big Mac is by far the chain's biggest hit. But standing in stark contrast to that sandwich are some wacky offerings. Which of these was *not* a real menu item from the fast-food behemoth?

A. McCrepe

B. McGratin Croquette

C. McLobster

D. McPizza

**5** M&Ms and Gatorade come in a rainbow of colors thanks to myriad artificial dyes. Researchers have found that one of these colors of dyes may help cure spinal cord injuries. Do you know which one?

**6** Which of the following has *not* been produced as a Jelly Belly flavor?

A. Bloody Mary

B. Denver Omelet

C. Pickle

D. Sausage

**4** A. You won't find a crepe on any Mickey D's menu past or present, but the other three have all been featured at some point. What's in a McGratin Croquette, you ask? The Japanese-market sandwich featured fried macaroni, shrimp, and mashed potatoes. Are you lovin' it?

**5** Blue. Researchers discovered that an injection of the dye Brilliant Blue G halted the chemical reaction that destroys spinal tissue after an injury. Better yet, after the dye was injected into rats paralyzed from spinal cord injuries, they were able to walk again. The only side effect? They temporarily turned blue.

**6** B. The other three have been rolled out as "specialty" flavors—although "special" may not be the word that comes to mind after tasting them. Pickle and Sausage are found in Bertie Bott's Every Flavor Beans, and Bloody Mary was a prototype "rookie" flavor that's no longer produced. What a shame!

**Which product was originally marketed as "Esteemed Brain Tonic and Intellectual Beverage"?**

A. Coca-Cola

B. Maxwell House coffee

C. Schweppes ginger ale

D. Smart Water

 **Clamshell, table, black trumpet, and golden needle are all types of what?**

A. Figs

B. Mushrooms

C. Pears

D. Snails

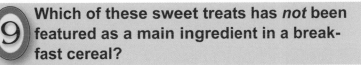 **Which of these sweet treats has *not* been featured as a main ingredient in a breakfast cereal?**

A. AirHeads

B. Ice cream

C. Raisinets

D. Willy Wonka's Nerds candy

Questions

F
O
O
D

&

D
R
I
N
K

**7** A. Coca-Cola was invented in Atlanta, Georgia, where it debuted in 1886 and sold for five cents a glass.

---

**8** B. If you see any of these varieties, feel free to yell, "There's a fungus among us!" (Although people might look at you funny.)

---

**9** C. Although sugar-happy tykes everywhere might think Raisin Bran could be improved by coating the raisins with chocolate, no such cereal has been created... yet. Cap'n Crunch's AirHeads Berries was produced by Quaker in 2003. In 1965 Kellogg's introduced Kream Krunch, which was filled with bits of freeze-dried ice cream. And the tangy flavor of Nerds candy was re-created in Nerds Cereal in the mid-1980s, with Ralston cleverly dividing the cereal box in half to feature a different flavor in each compartment, just like the candy box.

Answers

**10** Each year, people celebrate local food specialties with giant festivals. If you're tired of the same old chili cook-off or apple pie contest, you may want to check one of these out. All but one is a real festival—which is the odd man out?

A. Jelly Jam-boree

B. Turkey Testicle Festival

C. Waikiki SPAM Jam West

D. Virginia Roadkill Cook-off

 **11** True or false: Eating turkey makes people sleepy.

**12** Natural vanilla flavoring comes from which flower?

A. Calla lily

B. Dahlia

C. Orchid

D. Sweet pea

A. If you find yourself in the mood for some turkey testicles, drop by Huntley, Illinois, in November. For roadkill delicacies, head to Pocahontas County, West Virginia, in September. And if you like canned meat, you're in luck—every April, Hawaiians celebrate SPAM with a street fair. Alas, if you're looking to sample jellies and jams, you may have to start your own festival.

False. Turkey contains tryptophan—an amino acid that makes people sleepy—but it doesn't work unless it's consumed in large quantities.

C. Vanilla pods, or beans, are the fruit of the vanilla orchid—the only orchid plant that produces an edible fruit. Now, if only chocolate grew on trees.... Wait a minute—it does! Cacao pods, which are used to make chocolate, grow on small tropical trees called Theobroma cacao trees.

**Americans drink 13 billion gallons of soft drinks every year. Which of the following is *not* a real product?**

A. DraCola

B. EpilepsiPepsi

C. Leninade

D. Whooppee Soda

 **What is the only rock that is edible for humans?**

**Tofu (or *doufu,* as it would more accurately be spelled in China) is a staple of Asian cooking, and it has made inroads in North American cuisine because of its high protein and calcium content. It is made from soybeans; in fact, *dou* means "beans." But what does the *fu* translate as?**

A. Curd

B. Rotten

C. Silk

D. Vegan

**13** B. There's no such thing as EpilepsiPepsi. The other three were all actual soft drinks. DraCola was a cola product made for "Halloween fans of all ages" by Transylvania Imports. Leninade was humorously promoted with slogans like, "A taste worth standing in line for," and "A drink for the masses!" And Whooppee Soda was a ginger ale–flavored soda marketed as "The Bottled Joy."

**14** Salt. The mineral is essential to the body, but consuming too much is not good for you. No surprise there. But did you know that it can be deadly? An overdose of salt was a traditional method of suicide in ancient China.

**15** B. Mmmm-mm, "rotten beans." No wonder tofu has a bad rap!

*"As a child, my family's menu consisted of two choices: Take it or leave it."*

—Buddy Hackett

**16** Horse nettle, an ingredient that's sometimes found in tea, boasts which of the following benefits?

A. Acne combatant

B. Laxative

C. Pick-me-up

D. Sedative

 **17** Survey says: America's favorite pizza topping is pepperoni. Which of these ingredients is commonly found on pizza in Japan?

A. Cucumber

B. Mayonnaise

C. Pickled ginger

D. Rice

 **18** According to the U.S. Food and Drug Administration (FDA), most raw fruits and vegetables are completely fat-free. Which is the exception to this rule?

A. Bananas

B. Broccoli

C. Jicama

D. Plums

**16**  D. Horse nettle actually has nothing to do with horses, so PETA members have nothing to worry about. You might, though—horse nettle is a flowering weed whose unripe fruit is poisonous. The ripe fruit is not harmful, however, and when cooked it has mild sedative powers. Don't try this at home, kids!

---

 **17**  B. Squid, seaweed, corn, and bacon are also common toppings in Japan, and you'll even find delicacies like a mini–hot dog pizza on a Japanese Pizza Hut menu.

---

**18**  B. If you zeroed in on broccoli, you're correct. While the others have zero fat, broccoli has a whole—gasp—.5 grams per stalk. (Still pretty healthy, no? Doesn't that make you want to put down those nachos and buffalo wings?)

# GEEKERY

### 1 How long is a "score" of years?

A. 4 years

B. 7 years

C. 20 years

D. 80 years

### 2 How many millions make up a trillion?

### 3 How long does it take sunlight to reach Earth?

A. 8 seconds

B. 8 minutes

C. 8 hours

D. 8 days

C. Have you always wondered what Abraham Lincoln meant by "four score and seven years ago"? He was referring to the signing of the Declaration of Independence in 1776, which occurred 87 years—or four score and seven years—before his Gettysburg Address.

 There are one million millions in a trillion.

B. Traveling at the speed of, well, light, sunlight reaches our atmosphere eight minutes after leaving the sun.

## WHO KNEW?
It takes the sun between 225 million and 240 million years to complete one orbit around the galaxy. That's moving at a breakneck speed of 137 miles per second.

## 4. What does a pluviometer measure?

A. Cell tower strength

B. Hurricane strength

C. Radiation level

D. Rainfall amount

## 5. Where did Google get Its name?

A. It's the name of a galaxy discovered in 1998, the year the company was founded.

B. It's a variation of the term *googol,* a very large number (1 followed by 100 zeroes).

C. It's a type of sponge (symbolic of an ability to absorb large amounts of information).

D. It's gibberish; the founders of Google came up with the word after having a few cocktails.

## 6. Which of these superheroes debuted first?

A. Batman

B. Hulk

C. Spider-Man

D. Superman

**4** D. For when you want to know whether you should wear your Wellies or not.

**5** B. The amount of information that can be found with this search engine makes even a googol look small.

**6** D. Superman arrived from the planet Krypton in 1938. Batman was hot on his heels in 1939, but Spider-Man and the Hulk didn't make their debuts until 1962.

## WHO KNEW?
The magic word *shazam* in Captain Marvel comics is an acronym that stands for "Solomon's wisdom, Hercules's strength, Atlas's stamina, Zeus's power, Achilles's courage, and Mercury's speed."

Answers

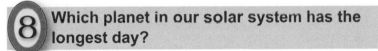

**7** How many letters of the alphabet are used in the Roman numeral system?

A. 6

B. 7

C. 8

D. 9

**8** Which planet in our solar system has the longest day?

A. Earth

B. Jupiter

C. Mercury

D. Venus

**9** Who was the founder of Scientology?

A. Arthur C. Clarke

B. Enrico Fermi

C. Steven Hawking

D. L. Ron Hubbard

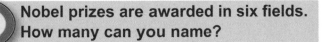

**10** Nobel prizes are awarded in six fields. How many can you name?

B. VII letters are used: I=1, V=5, X=10, L=50, C=100, D=500, and M=1,000.

 D. In fact, a day on Venus (equal to 243 Earth days) is longer than its year (225 Earth days).

9 D. In 1949, L. Ron Hubbard reportedly told fellow science-fiction writer Lloyd Eshbach, "I'd like to start a religion. That's where the money is." Despite the questionable intent, Scientology has enticed thousands into its fold.

10 Physics, chemistry, medicine or physiology, literature, peace, and economic science

*"A Life? Cool! Where can I download one of those?"*

—Unknown

**11** Which of the following is the chemical symbol for iron?

A. Fe

B. Ir

C. Tn

D. Zn

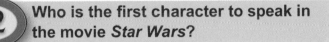 **12** Who is the first character to speak in the movie *Star Wars*?

BONUS! What does he or she say?

 **13** Can you match these mythical hybrids with their descriptions?

1. Centaur

2. Chimera

3. Minotaur

4. Satyr

5. Sphinx

A. Head and legs of a bull, torso of a man

B. Head and torso of a man, legs of a goat

C. Head and torso of a man, body of a horse

D. Head of a woman, body of a lion

E. Part lion, part goat, part serpent

Questions

**11** A. Ah, the periodic table. Good times.

___

 **12** C-3PO, the droid with the snazzy gold paint job, speaks first.

**BONUS!** "Did you hear that?" (He's talking to R2-D2, and "that" is the sound of the main reactor being shut down on Princess Leia's ship.)

___

**13** 1. C; 2. E; 3. A; 4. B; 5. D. Left off this list due to space constraints: the chiweenie (chihuahua/dachshund), cockapoo (cocker spaniel/poodle), and double doodle (labradoodle/goldendoodle).

*"Never make fun of the geeks. One day they will be your boss."*

—Unknown

**At what temperature does paper burn?**

A. 451°F

B. 507°F

C. 666°F

D. 800°F

 **What is the name of the world's fastest supercomputer?**

A. Maglev

B. Peregrine V

C. Roadrunner

D. Veyron TKR

 **Inky, Blinky, and Pinky are three of Pac-Man's four enemies. Who is the fourth?**

A. Clinky

B. Clyde

C. Dinky

D. Steve

 What color is Pac-Man?

**A.** So if you accidentally put the frozen pizza in the oven with its cardboard backing, you should be okay—as long as the temp is 450 degrees Fahrenheit or lower. (Still, it's best to pay attention and follow the directions, no?)

 **C.** IBM's hybrid supercomputer is twice as fast as Blue Gene, the world's second-fastest computer. Roadrunner can process 1,000 trillion operations per second. The computer is located at the Los Alamos National Laboratory in New Mexico.

 **B.** Clyde is the orange ghost. Blinky is red, Inky is blue, and Pinky is, well, pink.

 Yellow

**17** Why is Facebook's layout design blue?

A. The color is easier on the eyes than other colors, allowing users to spend more time on the site.

B. Facebook founder Mark Zuckerberg is colorblind.

C. Blue is the only color Zuckerberg knew how to code during Facebook's initial development.

D. Blue is Zuckerberg's favorite color.

**18** As Apple developed the Power Mac 7100 in the early 1990s, it used the name of a famous astronomer as a code name. Who was the astronomer?

A. Albert Einstein

B. Edwin Hubble

C. Carl Sagan

D. Clyde Tombaugh

*"There are 10 types of people in the world: those who understand binary, and those who don't."*

—Unknown

**17** B. Zuckerberg is colorblind. More specifically, he is red–green colorblind, and blue is the most vibrant color he can see.

---

**18** C. Sagan sued the company over the use of his name (and lost), but Apple decided to change the code name anyway, to "BHA." What did BHA stand for, you ask? "Butt-head astronomer."

## WHO KNEW?
The cosmos contains approximately 50 billion galaxies.

*"Science is the art of answering the tough questions and questioning the easy answers."*

—Unknown

# GRAB BAG

## 1 Which of the following is *not* a real beauty pageant?

A. Miss Klingon Empire

B. Miss Artificial Beauty

C. The Armpit Queen

D. Miss Michael Jackson

## 2 How many bathrooms does the White House have?

A. 22

B. 35

C. 50

D. 57

## 3 What is the best-selling car of all time?

D. The Miss Klingon Empire beauty pageant is held every September at Dragon*Con in Atlanta. A Miss Artificial Beauty pageant was held in Beijing, China, in 2004; each contestant had to present doctor-certified proof of her surgical enhancements. Old Spice deodorant sponsors an annual pageant and festival in Battle Mountain, Nevada, which was once dubbed "the armpit of America" by humorist Gene Weingarten of the *Washington Post*. Sweaty T-shirt contests, deodorant throws, and a "quick-draw" antiperspirant contest lead up to the selection of the Armpit Queen.

B. Encompassing approximately 55,000 square feet, the White House has 132 rooms, including 35 bathrooms and 16 family and guest rooms.

The Toyota Corolla. Since its 1966 debut, more than 37 million Corollas have been sold.

**4** **Jupiter, Mars, Mercury, Neptune, Pluto, and Venus are—or were—planets. (Sorry, Pluto.) What else do these names have in common?**

**5** **Which is *not* considered one of the seven holy virtues?**

A. Charity

B. Faith

C. Fortitude

D. Patience

**6** **What is the most commonly reported subject of people's dreams?**

A. Being chased

B. Falling/flying

C. Missing or failing an exam

D. Sex

GRAB BAG

Questions

65

Each is the name of a Roman god. Jupiter is the king of the gods; Mars is the god of war; Mercury is the messenger of the gods; Neptune is the god of the sea, earthquakes, and horses; Pluto is god of the dead and the Underworld; and Venus is the goddess of love and beauty.

 D. Whoever first uttered the adage "patience is a virtue" didn't know their holy virtues from a hole in the wall. The seven holy virtues are: faith, hope, charity, prudence, justice, temperance, and fortitude.

A. Being chased is by far the most-often reported theme of people's dreams. It's often interpreted as symbolic of feeling as though you are being pursued by events or unpleasant emotions in your daily life.

**7** The Japanese seem to have a yen for selling unusual products via vending machine—they sell more products this way than any other country. Which of these is *not* available for purchase in Japanese vending machines?

A. Designer condoms

B. Gasoline

C. Live rhinoceros beetles

D. Sake in preheated containers

**8** Alfred Kinsey, noted pioneer of sex research, spent years interviewing thousands of people to study human sexuality. He founded the Institute for Sex Research in 1947 at which university?

A. Indiana University

B. Northwestern University

C. The Ohio State University

D. University of Wisconsin

**9** What is the maximum number of characters allowed in a single tweet?

**7** B. In addition to live beetles (a popular pet for Japanese children), condoms, and warm drinks, Japanese vending machines have also been known to dispense fresh eggs, pornographic magazines, kerosene, and more. However, even though you may find a can of hot red beans for sale, one thing the vending machines won't give you is gas.

**8** A. Kinsey and his staff collected more than 18,000 interviews at a time when discussing sexuality was very much taboo in America. Some hailed him as a liberator of sexuality; others (including Billy Graham) vilified him as the direct cause of declining morals in Americans.

**9** 140

**WHO KNEW?**
There are 55 million tweets sent per day.

**10** What do Homer Simpson and Elvis Presley have in common?

 **11** How many astronauts have walked on the moon?

A. 9

B. 12

C. 14

D. 15

 **12** True or false: The modern brassiere was invented by a man.

 **13** Which sexy star has *not* been twice-crowned Sexiest Man Alive by *People* magazine?

A. George Clooney

B. Tom Cruise

C. Johnny Depp

D. Brad Pitt

*"The problem with beauty is that it's like being born rich and getting poorer."*

—Joan Collins

**10** They both have daughters named Lisa Marie.

**11** B. Between July 20, 1969, and December 19, 1972, six *Apollo* missions landed on the moon. Altogether, 12 astronauts spent time on lunar soil.

**12** False. Bras were invented in 1913 when American socialite Mary Phelps-Jacob tied two handkerchiefs together with ribbon. She patented the idea a year later. Modern cup sizes were introduced by Maidenform in 1928.

**13** B. Clooney (1997, 2006), Depp (2003, 2009), and Pitt (1995, 2000) have been anointed twice each, but Cruise has only earned the title once (1990).

**Benjamin Franklin is a member of 14 Halls of Fame. Which of the following is *not* one of them?**

A. Agricultural Hall of Fame

B. American Mensa Hall of Fame

C. International Swimming Hall of Fame

D. World Chess Hall of Fame

 **Stella Liebeck of Albuquerque, New Mexico, successfully sued McDonald's for gross negligence over what 1992 incident?**

A. Burned herself with hot coffee

B. Found a finger in her fries

C. Contracted salmonella poisoning from undercooked McNuggets

D. Slipped and fell on wet floor

 **What is Donald Duck's middle name?**

A. Buzz

B. Chesterfield

C. Fauntleroy

D. Fitzgerald

**A.** Among Franklin's myriad interests and talents, he was an enthusiastic and well-trained swimmer. When he was just a boy, he strapped boards to his hands in an effort to swim faster, effectively inventing the first swim paddles.

 **A.** The 79-year-old burned herself so severely that she needed skin grafts. Two years later, a jury awarded her more than $2.5 million, which an appeals court later reduced to $480,000. The sides eventually settled out of court for an undisclosed amount.

 **C.** "Fauntleroy" is a nice upper-class-sounding name, befitting a nephew of Scrooge McDuck, who has a fortune estimated at five billion quintiplitilion unptuplatillion multuplatillion impossibidillion fantasticatrillion dollars.

# MOVIE MANIA

**1** Who is Angelina Jolie's famous dad?

A. James Caan

B. George Hamilton

C. Harvey Keitel

D. Jon Voight

**2** Who is the oldest actor ever to win an Oscar?

A. George Burns

B. Kirk Douglas

C. Paul Newman

D. Christopher Plummer

**3** Superstar actor Johnny Depp and director Tim Burton have teamed up on eight films (so far). How many of them can you name?

**1** D. The two haven't always been on the best of terms, but they supposedly reconciled in 2010. Mom was actress Marcheline Bertrand.

 **2** D. Plummer was 82 years old when he scored the Best Supporting Actor statuette for his role in the 2011 film *Beginners.*

**3** *Edward Scissorhands* (1990), *Ed Wood* (1994), *Sleepy Hollow* (1999), *Charlie and the Chocolate Factory* (2005), *Corpse Bride* (2005), *Sweeney Todd* (2007), *Alice in Wonderland* (2010), and *Dark Shadows* (2012).

## WHO KNEW?

Just one actor (the 4'4" Deep Roy) portrayed all 165 Oompa Loompas in Tim Burton's *Charlie and the Chocolate Factory.*

**4** **Can you tell which of these is *not* the title of a real movie?**

A. *Cannibal Cousin and the Knife of Destiny*

B. *Sorority Babes in the Slimeball Bowl-O-Rama*

C. *Pumpkinhead II: Blood Wings*

D. *Mari-Cookie and the Killer Tarantula in 8 Legs to Love You*

**5** **What is the only X-rated movie ever to win an Academy Award for Best Picture?**

**6** **The James Bond series is famous for its gorgeous leading ladies. Can you match the Bond Girl with the movie in which she appeared?**

1. *Goldfinger*       A. Jinx Johnson

2. *You Only Live Twice*       B. Kissy Suzuki

3. *Quantum of Solace*       C. Pussy Galore

4. *Casino Royale*       D. Strawberry Fields

5. *Die Another Day*       E. Vesper Lynd

**4** A. Actress Linnea Quigly, known as the "Queen of Scream," starred in the other three (1988, 1994, and 1998, respectively), among other piquantly titled horror thrillers. The titles may be more scream-worthy than the movies!

**5** *Midnight Cowboy.* The movie, starring Dustin Hoffman and Jon Voight, took home the prize in 1969. Because of the growing stigma associated with X ratings, the film's rating was changed to R in 1971 without anything being changed or removed.

**6** 1. C; 2. B; 3. D; 4. E; 5. A.

### WHO KNEW?

When Pierce Brosnan played James Bond in *Goldeneye* (1995), his contract stated that he could not wear a tuxedo in any other film.

**7** There are more than 2,400 stars on the Hollywood Walk of Fame. Which of these major Hollywood superstars does *not* have one?

A. Clint Eastwood

B. Harrison Ford

C. Arnold Schwarzenegger

D. John Travolta

**8** In *Star Wars,* what is the name of Han Solo's spacecraft?

A. *Apollo*

B. *Enterprise*

C. *Millennium Falcon*

D. *Voyager*

**9** In the *Back to the Future* movies, at what speed is the DeLorean time machine activated?

A. 78 mph

B. 88 mph

C. 98 mph

D. 108 mph

**7** A. Go ahead—give Eastwood a star. It would probably make his day.

**8** C. The *Falcon*'s design was allegedly inspired by a hamburger, with the cockpit being an olive on the side. Mmmm-mm. Hungry?

**9** B. Hello? McFly? Is anybody home? Of course you knew that the flux capacitor kicks into gear at 88 miles per hour.

## WHO KNEW?

The head of Universal Pictures wanted *Back to the Future* to be titled *Spaceman from Pluto.* Producer Steven Spielberg thanked him for the "wonderful joke" and managed to retain the original title.

Answers

**10** Who played Indiana Jones's father in *Indiana Jones and the Temple of Doom*?

A. Sean Connery

B. James Garner

C. Gene Hackman

D. Peter O'Toole

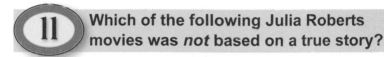**11** Which of the following Julia Roberts movies was *not* based on a true story?

A. *Charlie Wilson's War* (2007)

B. *Eat Pray Love* (2010)

C. *Erin Brockovich* (2000)

D. *Larry Crowne* (2011)

**12** Marilyn Monroe in a billowing white dress over a subway grate—who doesn't know that scene? But do you know what movie it's from?

A. *Gentlemen Prefer Blondes*

B. *How to Marry a Millionaire*

C. *The Seven-Year Itch*

D. *Some Like It Hot*

**10** A. Yep, James Bond himself was also Indy's dad. Director Steven Spielberg thought Connery was an obvious choice for the role, as Bond was an inspiration for Indiana's character.

---

**11** D. Don't get Charlie Wilson confused with Larry Crowne. Both movies costarred Tom Hanks; only one of them was the story of a real person (Wilson).

---

**12** C. The pose is so famous, in fact, that it was commemorated with a 26-foot-tall statue on Chicago's Magnificent Mile. Sadly, the statue was only a temporary display.

*"If you can make a girl laugh, you can make her do anything."*

—Marilyn Monroe

**13** Which famous *Saturday Night Live* alum wrote 2004's hit film *Mean Girls*?

A. Tina Fey

B. Ana Gasteyer

C. Amy Poehler

D. Maya Rudolph

 **14** Which Oscar-nominated action star is also a seasoned helicopter pilot and real-life hero?

A. Tom Cruise

B. Harrison Ford

C. John Travolta

D. Denzel Washington

 **15** "Teen movies" *The Breakfast Club, Ferris Bueller's Day Off,* and *Sixteen Candles* (all directed by John Hughes) were set in the suburbs of which metropolis?

A. Boston

B. Chicago

C. Los Angeles

D. Philadelphia

A. Gasteyer and Poehler each had a role in the film, but Fey wrote the script. Poehler played the mom of Rachel McAdams's mean-girl character, which was odd because in real life she's just seven years older than McAdams.

 B. Ford has twice rescued stranded hikers in his Bell 407 helicopter. In July 2000 he airlifted a hiker off Table Mountain in Idaho, and a year later he rescued a 13-year-old Boy Scout who had gotten lost in Yellowstone Park.

 B. It seems there was no place like home for Hughes, who grew up in Northbrook, Illinois, a suburb of Chicago.

**16** Which actor provides the voice of *Toy Story*'s Buzz Lightyear?

A. Tim Allen

B. Will Ferrell

C. Tom Hanks

D. Mike Myers

 **17** In 1999's *Office Space,* the meek and mumbly Milton is obsessed with which office supply?

A. Calculator

B. Scissors

C. Stapler

D. Wite-Out

**18** Which two actors starred in 2005's *Brokeback Mountain*?

**19** Which actress played Gertie in the movie *E.T. the Extra-Terrestrial*?

A. Drew Barrymore

B. Cameron Diaz

C. Gwyneth Paltrow

D. Reese Witherspoon

16 A. You're sure to recognize the other actors' voices from animated films as well: Will Ferrell plays Megamind, Tom Hanks is the voice of Buzz's pal Woody, and Mike Myers is Shrek.

17 C. Milton's all about his Swingline stapler. Well, that and burning down the building.

18 Jake Gyllenhaal and Heath Ledger. Both were nominated for Academy Awards.

19 A. Barrymore was just seven years old when she starred in the blockbuster movie.

### WHO KNEW?
*E.T.* director Steven Spielberg is Barrymore's godfather.

# MUSIC TO MY EARS

**1** By which name was Will Smith known during his early rap career?

 **BONUS!** Who was Smith's hip-hop collaborator (and occasional TV friend)?

**2** How many keys are on a standard piano keyboard?

**3** Which of the following singers got his stage name from a billboard advertising a hearing-aid retailer?

A. Sting
B. Prince
C. Bono
D. Moby

 Questions

**1** The Fresh Prince. He later starred on the TV show *The Fresh Prince of Bel-Air* (1990–96). At the time, few people would have predicted that the rapper would eventually be Oscar-nominated (*Ali,* 2001, and *The Pursuit of Happyness,* 2006).

**BONUS!** DJ Jazzy Jeff

**2** 88 (52 white, 36 black)

**3** C. As the story goes, Bono (Paul David Hewson) was inspired by a Dublin hearing-aid shop called Bono Vox—Latin for "good voice."

### WHO KNEW?
Bono is the only person who has been nominated for an Oscar, a Grammy, a Golden Globe, and a Nobel Prize.

**German composer Ludwig van Beethoven began to lose his sense of what when he was 28 years old?**

A. Hearing

B. Humor

C. Sight

D. Style

**5** A host of musical geniuses have gone to an early grave. Brian Jones (a founding member of the Rolling Stones), Jimi Hendrix, Janis Joplin, Jim Morrison, Kurt Cobain, and Amy Winehouse all passed away at the same young age. How old were they?

**6** Ozzy Osbourne became famous with which heavy metal band?

A. AC/DC

B. Black Sabbath

C. Iron Maiden

D. Judas Priest

**4** A. At around age 28, Beethoven developed a severe case of tinnitus and began to lose his hearing. This did not affect his ability to compose music, but it made conducting concerts increasingly difficult. According to one story, at the premiere of his Ninth Symphony when he was 54 years old, he had to be turned around to see the applause of the audience because he couldn't hear it.

**5** 27. If you're a rock star and you're about to turn 27, you might want to consider taking a year off.

**6** B. B is for Black Sabbath, but it's also for bat—as in the bat whose head Ozzy legendarily bit off when a fan tossed it onto the stage at a 1982 concert.

*"I got rabies shots for biting the head off a bat, but that's okay—the bat had to get Ozzy shots."*

—Ozzy Osbourne

**7** Put these *American Idol* winners in order from earliest to most recent.

A. Kris Allen

B. Fantasia Barrino

C. David Cook

D. Jordin Sparks

E. Carrie Underwood

 Which *American Idol* contestant has won an Academy Award?

 **8** What eventually killed the old lady who swallowed the fly?

A. A cow

B. A fly

C. A horse

D. A moose

**9** True or false: Michael Jackson's *Thriller* video was nominated for an Academy Award.

**7** B (Season 3), E (Season 4), D (Season 6), C (Season 7), A (Season 8)

 **BONUS!** Jennifer Hudson (Best Supporting Actress 2006, *Dreamgirls*)

---

**8** C. A horse, of course!

---

**9** False. It wasn't nominated, but producers made sure it was eligible by giving it a one-week theatrical release in 1983, opening for the Disney movie *Fantasia.* Parents weren't too thrilled about their toddlers getting an eyeful of zombie action.

*"He has Van Gogh's ear for music."*

—Billy Wilder

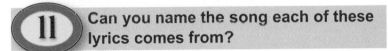

**10** Which country singer is known as the Man in Black?

A. Clint Black

B. Garth Brooks

C. Johnny Cash

D. Hank Williams

**11** Can you name the song each of these lyrics comes from?

A. "Thunderbolt and lightning, very, very frightening."

B. "A singer in a smoky room, a smell of wine and cheap perfume."

C. "Hands, touching hands, reaching out, touching me, touching you."

D. "Well, I know that you're in love with him, 'cause I saw you dancin' in the gym."

E. "You start to scream, but terror takes the sound before you make it."

**12** Who is the Greek god of music?

A. Apollo

B. Dionysus

C. Hermes

D. Zeus

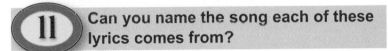

MUSIC TO MY EARS

Questions

**10** C. Cash has been inducted into the Country Music Hall of Fame, the Rock and Roll Hall of Fame, the Gospel Music Hall of Fame, and the Rockabilly Hall of Fame.

**11** A. "Bohemian Rhapsody" (Queen);
B. "Don't Stop Believin'" (Journey);
C. "Sweet Caroline" (Neil Diamond);
D. "American Pie" (Don McLean); E. "Thriller" (Michael Jackson).

**12** A. Apollo was not only the god of music—he was also the god of healing, the sun, and poetry, to name a few. If you got this question right, lift your glass to (B) Dionysus, god of wine, parties, and festivals.

**13** Which legendary jazz musician was known as "Satchmo"?

A. Duke Ellington

B. Charlie Parker

C. Glenn Miller

D. Louis Armstrong

 **14** John Williams, winner of multiple Oscars, Grammys, Golden Globes, and Emmy awards, and composer of some of the most recognizable film scores in history, also composed the theme music for three of these four events. Which of the following did *not* at one time have a theme composed by Williams?

A. Olympics

B. Academy Awards show

C. NBC Nightly News

D. NBC Sunday Night Football

**15** What do rock 'n' roller Jerry Lee Lewis and master of the macabre Edgar Allen Poe have in common?

D. When Armstrong was a child, his friends called him Satchelmouth because they thought his mouth was as large as a satchel. (He was also sometimes called Gatemouth. With friends like that, who needs enemies?) A music journalist mispronounced the moniker, shortening it to "Satchmo." Armstrong loved the name and quickly adopted it.

 B. Although Williams is the second-most-nominated person in Academy Awards history—47 nods as of 2012—he has never composed the music for the show. (In case you're wondering, Walt Disney has the most nominations, with 59.)

15 Each married his own 13-year-old cousin.

**16** Many famous rock 'n' roll bands went by different names before they made it big. Can you identify the former names of these bands?

1. The Beatles

2. Journey

3. KISS

4. The Rolling Stones

5. U2

A. Feedback; The Hype

B. Golden Gate Rhythm Section

C. The Pendletones

D. Satan's Jesters

E. Wicked Lester

**17** The Woodstock Music and Art Festival was held August 15–18, 1969, not in Woodstock but in Bethel, New York, 40 miles away. Woodstock was supposed to host the festival, but when rumors spread that attendance could reach a million people, the city backed out. Dairy farmer Max Yasgur saved the concert by hosting it in a field at his farm. What crop was growing in that field?

A. Alfalfa

B. Cabbage

C. Corn

D. Marijuana

**16** 1. C; 2. B; 3. E; 4. D; 5. A.

**17** A. Alfalfa is the answer, but the free-spirited flower children who attended the concert might have preferred one of the other options.

*"I think you people have proven something to the world: . . . that a half million young people can get together and have three days of fun and music and have nothing but fun and music, and God bless you for it!"*

—Max Yasgur

# PUB TIME

 **True or false: Wine has a higher alcohol content than beer.**

 **Which country is the home of Grolsch lager?**

A. Austria

B. Belgium

C. Germany

D. The Netherlands

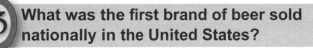 **What was the first brand of beer sold nationally in the United States?**

A. Budweiser

B. Coors

C. Miller

D. Pabst Blue Ribbon

**1** True. Table wine contains about 12 percent alcohol, while most regular beers have just 5 percent alcohol.

**2** D. The Dutch brewery is almost four centuries old—it was founded in 1615.

**3** A. PBR was the first to be brewed (Pabst Brewing Company was founded in 1844), but Bud was the first to be sold nationally. After Adolphus Busch pioneered the use of pasteurization, refrigerated railcars, and a network of icehouses in the 1870s, Anheuser–Busch became the first company to distribute beer across the country.

## WHO KNEW?
During World War II, American breweries were required to allocate 15 percent of their production for military use.

**Which of the following sizes of wine bottles is the largest?**

A. Fifth

B. Magnum

C. Methuselah

D. Nebuchadnezzar

 **What flavor is the liqueur Cointreau?**

A. Cherry

B. Coffee

C. Orange

D. Prickly pear

**What do screwdrivers and bloody marys have in common? Vodka, of course! This colorless alcohol hails from Russia, where its original name, *zhiznennaia voda,* means what?**

A. "Beauty and wellness"

B. "Healing water"

C. "Joy"

D. "Water of life"

 Questions

**4** D. A nebuchadnezzer holds the equivalent of 20 bottles of wine.

---

**5** C. How do you pronounce *Cointreau,* anyway? Unless you speak French or bartenderese, you may stumble over this one. It's pronounced *kwahn-TRO.*

---

 **6** D. The name was later shortened, and *voda* ("water") morphed into *vodka,* which is the diminutive form of the word. Literally translated, *vodka* means "dear little water." Aww.

*"Beer is proof that God loves us and wants us to be happy."*

—Benjamin Franklin

**(7)** Pombe, a form of beer from east Africa, is made by mashing a certain type of fruit with one's bare feet and then burying it in a cask. What fruit is used?

A. Apples

B. Bananas

C. Kumquats

D. Pomegranates

**(8)** What type of alcohol is typically used to make a daiquiri?

A. Brandy

B. Rum

C. Tequila

D. Whiskey

**(9)** What is added to tomato juice to make a bloody maria?

A. Beer

B. Rum

C. Tequila

D. Vodka

B. History shows that humans will make alcohol from any ingredients available, and bananas are no exception.

---

 B. The main ingredients in a traditional daiquiri are rum, lime juice, and sugar. The list of flavor variations can be as long as the line at a swim-up bar.

---

C. Don't confuse a bloody maria with a bloody mary, which uses vodka. Both are tasty with a splash of hot sauce and a celery garnish!

*"It is well to remember that there are five reasons for drinking: the arrival of a friend; one's present or future thirst; the excellence of the wine; or any other reason."*

—Latin proverb

**10** The phrase "mind your Ps and Qs" originally meant to be careful not to overimbibe. What do "P" and "Q" stand for?

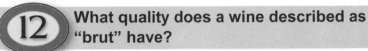

**11** What is a crapulous person full of?

A. Alcohol

B. Food

C. Gas

D. Lies

**12** What quality does a wine described as "brut" have?

A. Dry

B. Expensive

C. Red

D. Sweet

**13** In which state is Jack Daniel's whiskey made?

A. Kentucky

B. Ohio

C. Tennessee

D. West Virginia

**10** Pints and quarts

---

**11** A. Crapulous people can also be full of food (and, it's likely, gas), but the definition of the word is "sick from excessive indulgence in liquor" or "drunken; given up to excess in drinking; characterized by intemperance."

---

**12** A. "Brut" is a term for dry (that is, not sweet) sparkling wine or champagne.

---

**13** C. Many people know the brand simply as "Jack" (as in, "I'll have a Jack and Coke" or "Gimmee a shot of Jack"). The whiskey comes in a square bottle, reportedly because more than 100 years ago, Mr. Jack Daniel claimed that a square shooter like himself should have a square bottle.

**14** *Dipsophobia* is the fear of what?

A. Drinking

B. Eating

C. Partying

D. Passing out

 **15** Who sings the popular party song "Red Solo Cup"?

 **16** What country is Red Stripe lager originally from?

A. The Bahamas

B. Costa Rica

C. Haiti

D. Jamaica

 **17** Fill in the blank: Grapes are to wine as _____ is to tequila.

A. Agave

B. Cactus

C. Corn

D. Juniper

A. Dipsophobic people are afraid of drinking. Some people with this condition are specifically afraid of drinking alcohol; others fear drinking any liquid.

 Toby Keith. The song is featured on Keith's 2011 album *Clancy's Tavern.* The song isn't an award-winner, but it sure is a crowd pleaser: According to Keith, the song is "so stupid it's good."

 D. It's from Jamaica, mon, and it carries the laid-back vibe of the island with it. Just check out the Red Stripe website, which joyously proclaims, "Red Stripe! It's beer! Hooray Beer!"

A. Wine is made from grapes; tequila is made from the fermented juice of the blue agave plant.

**18** James Bond is known for his preference for vodka martinis, shaken, not stirred; Homer Simpson can't get enough Duff beer; and *Sex and the City*'s Carrie Bradshaw enjoys a pink Cosmo as much as the next girl. What drink does *Mad Men*'s Don Draper mix up in his swanky ad agency office?

A. Gimlet

B. Old-fashioned

C. Rob Roy

D. Whiskey sour

 **19** Where is the oldest tavern in America located?

A. Boston, MA

B. Jamestown, VA

C. Philadelphia, PA

D. Providence, RI

**20** Winston Churchill's mother is credited with inventing what cocktail?

A. Gimlet

B. Gin Rickey

C. Manhattan

D. Rob Roy

B. Drinking during the day? Why not? If you're the boss, you can do what you want. And Don Draper wants an old-fashioned, thank you very much.

A. Established in 1795, Boston's Bell in Hand Tavern is the longest continuously operating tavern in America. Founded by town crier Jimmy Wilson, the Bell in Hand still serves frosty mugs and food to an often full house. Famous customers at the bar have included Paul Revere and President William McKinley.

C. The manhattan got its name from the Manhattan Club in New York City, where it was first concocted. Legend has it that Lady Randolph Churchill (Winston's mother) commissioned the cocktail in 1874 at a banquet that was held in honor of presidential candidate Samuel J. Tilden.

# SPORTS OF ALL SORTS

**1** Which sports figure has *not* been featured on a Wheaties cereal box?

A. "Stone Cold" Steve Austin (professional wrestler)

B. Rulon Gardner (Olympic Greco–Roman wrestler)

C. Joe Paterno (college football coach)

D. Esther Williams (swimmer; actress)

**2** Which NFL team has won the most Super Bowls?

**3** Which famous athlete not-so-humbly claimed, "When you are as great as I am, it's hard to be humble"?

A. Muhammad Ali

B. Charles Barkley

C. Reggie Jackson

D. Babe Ruth

Questions

**1** B. Gardner never muscled his way onto the box, but Austin, Paterno, and Williams graced breakfast tables across America in 1999, 2003, and 1959, respectively.

---

**2** Pittsburgh Steelers (six): 1975, 1976, 1979, 1980, 2006, and 2009

---

 **3** A. Not only could the champion boxer float like a butterfly and sting like a bee, but he was also a champion boaster.

*"At home I am a nice guy, but I don't want the world to know. Humble people, I've found, don't get very far."*

—Muhammad Ali

**4** Which of the following pro football–playing brothers are twins?

A. Ronde and Tiki Barber

B. Eli and Peyton Manning

C. Adrian and Mike Peterson

D. Byron and Brian Westbrook

 **5** The 1974 World Heavyweight Championship boxing match in Zaire between George Foreman and Muhammad Ali was known by what name?

 **6** What is golfer Arnold Palmer's nickname?

A. The Golden Bear

B. The Great White Shark

C. The Hawk

D. The King

 **7** Which three horse races make up the Triple Crown?

A. The Barber boys are identical twins—and they're not related to the NFL's other Barber brothers, Dominique and Marion.

 "The Rumble in the Jungle." The bout was stopped in the eighth round, with Ali handing Foreman his first-ever defeat.

 D. The most popular golfer of all time, Arnie is known by millions of fans (dubbed "Arnie's Army") simply as "The King." If you've heard the other monikers but can't tie them to their owners, here you go: the Golden Bear is Jack Nicklaus, the Great White Shark is Greg Norman, and the Hawk was Ben Hogan.

7 The Kentucky Derby, the Preakness Stakes, and the Belmont Stakes

**8** **What was the original name of the Nike corporation?**

A. Apollo Sports

B. Blue Ribbon Sports

C. Gold Medal Sports

D. Olympia Sports

 **9** **Which sport features players using a cesta to throw a pelota at speeds of more than 120 miles per hour?**

A. Jai alai

B. Racquetball

C. Skeet shooting

D. Squash

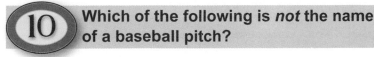 **10** **Which of the following is *not* the name of a baseball pitch?**

A. Forkball

B. Gyroball

C. Knuckleball

D. Shovelball

B. In 1971 the founders of the small sports-shoe business Blue Ribbon Sports in Beaverton, Oregon, were searching for a catchy, energetic company name. They settled on Nike, the name of the Greek goddess of victory. And victorious they were: Nike is now the largest sports-wear manufacturer in the world.

---

 A. Jai alai originated in Spain and is not common in the United States, although it does have a large following in Miami. Because pelotas hit the court walls at such high speeds, each has an average life of only about 20 minutes before its cover splits and it needs to be replaced.

---

D. A forkball is a type of fastball, and a knuckleball is a unique trick pitch that's more pushed than thrown. A gyroball is a type of pitch in which the ball spins on an axis, much like a spiral pass in football.

 **What does NASCAR stand for?**

 **Which baseball team was at the center of the scandal in the film *Eight Men Out*?**

A. Boston Red Sox

B. Brooklyn Dodgers

C. Chicago Cubs

D. Chicago White Sox

 **The NBA's logo features a silhouette of a player dribbling a basketball. Which basketball legend is the image modeled on?**

A. Rick Barry

B. Julius Erving

C. Michael Jordan

D. Jerry West

 **What was Babe Ruth's real name?**

*"We didn't lose the game; we just ran out of time."*

—Vince Lombardi

 115

**SPORTS OF ALL SORTS**

**11** National Association of Stock Car Auto Racing. That's contrary to the old joke that says NASCAR was founded when a redneck saw a nice car and said, "Man, that's a naaas car!"

**12** D. The 1919 scandal, known as the "Black Sox scandal," occurred when eight members of the White Sox conspired with mobsters to intentionally lose the World Series to the Cincinnati Reds.

**13** D. Although the NBA declines to comment on the identity of the player, the logo's designer is not so reserved. He says he originally designed 40 or 50 options, every one of which featured "Mr. Clutch" (West).

**14** George Herman Ruth

**15** Who was the first major-league base-ball player to have his number retired?

A. Ty Cobb

B. Lou Gehrig

C. Jackie Robinson

D. Babe Ruth

 **16** Which tennis player was viciously stabbed while playing a match in Hamburg, Germany, in 1993?

A. Steffi Graff

B. Magdalena Maleeva

C. Gabriela Sabatini

D. Monica Seles

 **17** Who scored the winning goal for the U.S. men's hockey team in the "Miracle on Ice" game against the Soviet Union in the 1980 Olympics?

A. Mike Eruzione

B. Mark Johnson

C. Rob McClanahan

D. Dave Silk

B. Gehrig wore number 4 for the New York Yankees. The team retired his number on July 4, 1939, after he announced his retirement and diagnosis of amyotrophic lateral sclerosis (ALS).

---

 D. An obsessed fan of Steffi Graf stabbed Seles in the back with a 9-inch boning knife during a quarterfinals match against Maleeva. Seles recovered from her wounds after a few weeks, but she didn't return to competitive tennis for two years.

---

 A. Eruzione was the team captain. His winning goal—one of the most played highlights in American sports—was voted the greatest highlight of all time by ESPN viewers in 2008.

**18** What is an NBA player deemed to be if he is awarded the Maurice Podoloff Trophy?

A. Defensive Player of the Year

B. Most Improved Player

C. Most Valuable Player

D. Rookie of the Year

**19** Football great Joe Namath once wore what unexpected item in a television commercial?

**20** Two Baseball Hall of Famers were once members of the Harlem Globetrotters: Two-time Cy Young Award–winner Bob Gibson, who attended college on a basketball scholarship and played with the Globetrotters before joining the St. Louis Cardinals, was one. Who was the other?

A. Reggie Jackson

B. Fergie Jenkins

C. Bob Lemon

D. Willie Mays

**18** C. Podoloff was the first president of the NBA and is the namesake of the league's Most Valuable Player Award.

**19** Pantyhose. The football legend donned a pair of Beauty Mist pantyhose to show that they could "make any legs look like a million dollars."

**20** B. The 6'5" Arthur Ferguson "Fergie" Jenkins played more than 80 games with the Globetrotters during the baseball off-seasons from 1967 to 1969.

## WHO KNEW?
Pope John Paul II was named an honorary member of the Harlem Globetrotters in 2000.

# TELEVISION TURN-ON

**1** What is the name of the holiday celebration coined on the TV show *Seinfeld*?

**BONUS!** Instead of a Christmas tree, what is put up for this holiday?

**2** Jon Stewart has made a global impact as host of *The Daily Show* on Comedy Central, and the show has helped launch the careers of several former cast members as well. Which of the following funny folks did *not* get his or her start on *The Daily Show*?

A. Steve Carrell

B. Stephen Colbert

C. Ed Helms

D. Amy Sedaris

**1** Festivus. Those looking to celebrate the "Festivus for the Rest of Us" should plan on the traditional "Airing of Grievances" and "Feats of Strength," in which the head of household must be pinned in a wrestling match.

*BONUS!*

An unadorned aluminum pole

**2** D. The actress, comedian, and author has appeared on Stewart's show as a guest, but she was never a regular contributor.

*"If you don't stick to your values when they're being tested, they're not values. They're hobbies."*

—Jon Stewart

**3** Who is CNN anchor Anderson Cooper's famous mother?

**4** Who cohosted the first season of *American Idol* alongside Ryan Seacrest?

A. Brian Dunkleman

B. Jason Kennedy

C. Ben Lyons

D. Catt Sadler

**5** Which Hollywood A-listers portrayed Rachel Green's sisters on *Friends*?

A. Amy Adams and Kate Hudson

B. Cameron Diaz and Drew Barrymore

C. Christina Applegate and Reese Witherspoon

D. Heather Graham and Rachel McAdams

**6** By what name did the core group of friends refer to themselves on the series *Buffy the Vampire Slayer* (1997–2003)?

A. The Badanovs

B. The Felix Faith

C. The Scooby Gang

D. The Underdog Squad

Fashion designer Gloria Vanderbilt. Cooper has a pretty impressive lineage: He is the great-great-great-grandson of nineteenth-century railroad tycoon Cornelius Vanderbilt.

 A. Dunkleman left the show after the first season with his career in ruins. Seacrest went on to become an entertainment mogul.

 C. Applegate played Rachel's sister Amy, and Witherspoon played Jill.

C. Buffy, Willow, Xander, and Giles formed the core of the Scooby Gang, or the Scoobies. The spooky goings-on in Sunnydale, California, influenced today's vampire, werewolf, and supernatural craze.

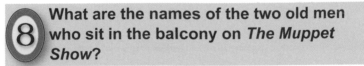

**7** Tom Hanks has been nominated five times for a Best Actor Academy Award and has won twice. But he got his big break on this sitcom in the 1980s:

A. *Bosom Buddies*

B. *Cheers*

C. *My Two Dads*

D. *Who's the Boss?*

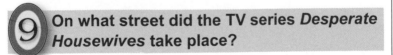

**8** What are the names of the two old men who sit in the balcony on *The Muppet Show*?

A. Aspin and Ludsthorp

B. Chilton and Gerard

C. Hawkins and Nigel

D. Waldorf and Statler

**9** On what street did the TV series *Desperate Housewives* take place?

A. Hydrangea Terrace

B. Magnolia Drive

C. Peachtree Circle

D. Wisteria Lane

**7** A. No amount of awards can ever erase the image of Tom Hanks dressed in drag.

**8** D. The ornery octogenarians enjoy heckling the other Muppets from the best seats in the house. Their names are based on hotels in New York: the Waldorf–Astoria and the Statler Hilton.

**9** D. Wisteria Lane may look like a "real" street, but in fact it's a set on the Universal Studios lot. Its real name is Colonial Street, and it has served as a location for many other film and TV productions, including *Leave It to Beaver* and *Buffy the Vampire Slayer.* From the 'burbs to the Hellmouth— that *is* magical.

**Match these TV series to the cities in which they are set.**

1. *CSI: Crime Scene Investigation*   A. Las Vegas
2. *Grey's Anatomy*   B. New York City
3. *House*   C. Princeton,
4. *Law & Order* (the original)   New Jersey
5. *NCIS*   D. Seattle
   E. Washington,
   D.C.

 **BONUS!** There have been four American spin-offs of the original *Law & Order*. How many can you name?

**Over the course of *The Simpsons*, Homer's career path has zigged and zagged. Which of the following job descriptions would *not* show up on his résumé?**

A. Astronaut
B. Avon lady
C. Carny
D. Monorail conductor

**10** Answer: 1. A; 2. D; 3. C; 4. B; 5. E.

**BONUS!** *Special Victims Unit, Criminal Intent, Trial by Jury,* and *L.A.* Versions of the show have also been produced in Russia, France, and the United Kingdom.

---

**11** B. Homer's primary job is as a nuclear power plant safety inspector, but he has tried his hand at many other trades during his long and distinguished career. In addition to astronaut, carny, and monorail conductor, he has been a butler, food critic, garbage commissioner, Kwik-E-Mart employee, and village oaf—to name a few.

## WHO KNEW?
Homer Simpson's e-mail address is Chunkylover53@aol.com.

**Which Oscar-nominated actor is rumored to have hated the '80s TV show he starred on so much that he lit his underwear on fire in an attempt to get fired?**

A. George Clooney

B. Johnny Depp

C. Tom Hanks

D. Will Smith

**How long did Kim Kardashian and Kris Humphries's marriage last?**

A. 22 days

B. 52 days

C. 72 days

D. 92 days

***South Park* cocreator Trey Parker has said that he named Cartman's mom after his former fiancée. What is her name?**

A. Elaine

B. Liane

C. Lisa

D. LuAnne

**12**

B. When Depp joined the cast of *21 Jump Street* in 1987, he did so believing it would be for only one season, but when the show became a hit he was stuck. Eager to be taken more seriously, Depp got creative in trying to escape his contract, but it took four long seasons before he was finally free to leave. He apparently got over his distaste for the role, however, and good-naturedly made a cameo in the 2012 movie based on the series.

**13**

C. Although the wedding event was called a fairy tale, the marriage was anything but. After their reported $10 million tele-vised nuptials in 2011, the reality-show celebutante and NBA player quickly called it quits.

**14**

B. According to Parker, after his fiancée cheated on him, he immortalized her by naming the cartoon's most promiscuous character after her. Ouch.

Answers

**15** Which of these actors was never a member of the *Saturday Night Live* cast?

A. Alec Baldwin

B. Robert Downey Jr.

C. Will Ferrell

D. Adam Sandler

**16** Which future TV star was pulled onstage to dance with Bruce Springsteen in the music video for "Dancing in the Dark"?

A. Courteney Cox

B. Calista Flockhart

C. Teri Hatcher

D. Sarah Jessica Parker

**17** Put these reality shows in the order in which they debuted, first to last:

A. *American Idol*

B. *Dancing with the Stars*

C. *The Real World*

D. *Survivor*

E. *Top Chef*

**15** A. As of 2012, Baldwin has hosted *SNL* a record 16 times, but he was never a cast member.

---

**16** A. It looks like an impromptu performance, but in fact Cox was cast for the part by director Brian de Palma. On Springsteen's *Born in the U.S.A.* tour, however, the thrill of a lifetime was real: The Boss selected a young woman at random to be his dance partner at each concert.

---

**17** C (1992); D (2000); A (2002); B (2005); E (2006)

*"There's something to be said for embracing who you are."*

—*Survivor* host Jeff Probst

# WHERE IN THE WORLD

**①** **Where is the Colosseum located?**

A. Athens

B. Florence

C. Jerusalem

D. Rome

**②** **What's the only city in the world that's located on two continents?**

**③** **In what country is the world's tallest building?**

A. Malaysia

B. Saudi Arabia

C. Tokyo

D. United Arab Emirates

**1** D. The arena was built in 80 A.D. and was primarily a venue where Romans enjoyed the spectacles of gladiator battles and wild animal fights.

 **2** Istanbul, Turkey. Istanbul flanks the Bosporus Strait between Asia and Europe. (See, all those years of studying for the geography bee finally paid off!)

**3** D. At 2,722.57 feet, the Burj Khalifa in Dubai, UAE, is the tallest man-made structure in the world. It was completed in 2010.

## WHO KNEW?

Plans have been announced for two new buildings that would be even taller than the Burj Khalifa: Kingdom Tower in Saudi Arabia and Azerbaijan Tower in Azerbaijan.

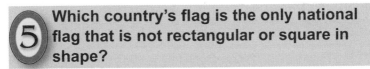

**4** Ever hear of Boring, Maryland? How about Nimrod, Minnesota, or Boogertown, North Carolina? Believe it or not, these are real towns. Which of the following towns *won't* you find on a map?

A. Accident, Maryland

B. Bird-on-a-Wire, Washington

C. Toad Suck, Alabama

D. Wide Awake, Colorado

**5** Which country's flag is the only national flag that is not rectangular or square in shape?

A. Bhutan

B. Cyprus

C. Libya

D. Nepal

 **BONUS!** What color is it?

**6** Where can Io, Europa, Ganymede, and Callisto be found?

**4** B. You can stop in Accident, Toad Suck, or Wide Awake on your next cross-country road trip, but there's no such place as Bird-on-a-Wire.

---

**5** D. The Nepalese flag is shaped like two pennants stacked vertically.

**BONUS!** Crimson with a blue border, with a white sun-and-crescent on top and a white sun on the bottom.

---

**6** Orbiting Jupiter. They are the four largest of Jupiter's 66 moons.

**7** The island of Murano is located off the coast of Venice, Italy. What is it best known for?

A. Glassblowing

B. Metal forging

C. Pottery

D. Wineries

**8** What is the longest river in the world?

A. Amazon

B. Mississippi

C. Nile

D. Yangtze

**9** What is the smallest country in the world?

A. Liechtenstein

B. Monaco

C. Nauru

D. Vatican City

**10** Where is the only place that the American flag flies continuously and is never raised or lowered?

**7** A. The island's reputation as a center for artisan glass dates back to the 13th century.

**8** C. At 4,132 miles long, the Nile, which starts in Lake Victoria and flows north through Africa all the way to the Mediterranean Sea, is more than 100 miles longer than its closest competitor (the Amazon, in South America).

**9** D. At just .2 mile in area, the tiny country has a population of less than 800 people. It is surrounded by Rome and is the spiritual center of Roman Catholicism.

**10** The moon

**Which four presidents appear on Mount Rushmore?**

 **Speaking of Mount Rushmore, there's another memorial being carved into a mountain in the Black Hills of South Dakota. Who is the subject of this monument?**

A. Chief Joseph

B. Crazy Horse

C. Geronimo

D. Sitting Bull

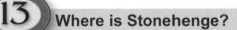 **Where is Stonehenge?**

A. England

B. Ireland

C. Scotland

D. Wales

 **Which of the following is *not* the capital of a U.S. state?**

A. Albany

B. Carson City

C. Dubuque

D. Tallahassee

11 George Washington, Thomas Jefferson, Theodore Roosevelt, and Abraham Lincoln

12 B. The Crazy Horse memorial has been under construction since 1948. When it's finally finished it will be the largest statue in the world—more than 600 feet long and almost as tall.

13 A. Okay, we know *where* the prehistoric monument is (Wiltshire County, south-west England), but do we know *what* it is? Not really. The best guesses include a temple for sun worship, a healing center, a burial site, or a huge calendar.

14 C. Albany is the capital of New York, Carson City of Nevada, and Tallahassee of Florida, but Des Moines—not Dubuque—is the capital of Iowa.

**15** What does the ZIP in ZIP code stand for?

 **16** Which American city is known for dying its river green for St. Patrick's Day every year?

A. Chicago

B. Cleveland

C. New Orleans

D. New York

 **17** In what Spanish city does the famous "running of the bulls" festival take place each July?

A. Barcelona

B. Madrid

C. Pamplona

D. Valencia

 **18** Which line of latitude—the Tropic of Cancer or the Tropic of Capricorn—is north of the equator, and which is south?

**15** Zoning Improvement Plan. The United States Postal Service established this system in 1963.

**16** A. Although some would argue that the river is always a murky shade of green, 40 pounds of nontoxic vegetable dye transform it into a bright, Irish green for the city's annual St. Patty's Day parade.

**17** C. Olé! Unlike bullfights, which are open only to professionals, anyone age 18 or older is welcome to participate in the *encierro* (running of the bulls).

**18** The Tropic of Cancer is north of the equator, and the Tropic of Capricorn is south of it. An easy way to remember this is to note that *Cancer* comes before *Capricorn* alphabetically, and it is above it on a map as well.

**You can get your kicks at three of these attractions on Route 66. Which one is *not* located along the scenic roadway?**

A. Cadillac Ranch

B. Eiffel Tower replica

C. Sidewalk Highway

D. World's largest ketchup bottle

**All your life you've heard that the United States of America has 50 states. Hold that thought: Technically, the United States comprises only 46 states: Four states designate themselves commonwealths. Can you name them?**

**The Four Corners is the only place in the United States where four states come together at one location. Which are the four states?**

**19**

B. When it was built, Route 66 connected Chicago and Los Angeles. Kitschy attractions and national landmarks such as the Grand Canyon, Meteor Crater, and the Petrified Forest abound along the way. If you're looking for the Eiffel Tower replica, however, you'll have to take a detour to Paris . . . Tennessee.

---

**20**

Kentucky, Massachusetts, Pennsylvania, and Virginia. What's the difference between a state and a commonwealth, you ask? Well, nothing. Constitutionally speaking, there's no difference at all.

---

**21**

Arizona, Colorado, New Mexico, and Utah. (Who ever said you can't be in more than one place at the same time?)